DANIELLE Y. MCLEAN

Table of Contents

Dedication

I dedicate this book to my daughter, Brandi Danielle McLean. I'm tearing up even thinking about you. You were and still are so special to me. I thank you for allowing me to share your story with the world. I remember you telling me that if telling your story would help others then you were fine with it. Daddy and I have coined you our "Golden Child". I know that this journey was not easy for any of us, but through it all our love one for another has been strengthened. Mommy and Daddy are so Godly proud of you. Each day you are still making decisions that glorify God! I thank God that He entrusted you into our care. We love you Baby Girl, and we will continue being your greatest cheerleaders. Make God proud and share who He has predestined you to be with the world. Continue to sing His praises!!!

Special Thank You's

First of all, I thank you God for always being with me. When I could not get my words or thoughts together You understood everything. You counseled me. You comforted me. You consoled me. I thank You for being there, never leaving me, never forsaking me, and never forgetting about me. I am grateful that You always remain the same with me, correcting me, giving me instructions every day, and for being the Best Listener. I thank You for putting people strategically in our lives at the right time to assist us and to speak life to us.

Secondly, thank you to my husband, Pastor Tim McLean. Babe, for sure we are a team, and I thank you for the wisdom and strength that you walk in. I thank you for having ears that hear God's voice. So many times you told me what God said and that was what we did. Each and every time God did exactly what He said He would do. We have endured this journey together, and I thank you from the bottom of my heart for being the head of our household. I love you!

To Robertha McLean (Grandma) - Thank you for being a listening ear to our daughter and for constantly steering her in the right direction to obey the Will of God. We appreciate you for loving her and us unconditionally. We love you Ma McLean!

To Mrs. Iris Primrose – Thank you for being a prayer warrior and standing on the wall for my baby girl's deliverance. Thank you for loving her as if though she were your very own. Thank you for being available and having a listening ear to God for Him to give you the confession that I still say to this day. I love you Mrs. Primrose!

To Mrs. Tanea Johnson and Mrs. Tanya Turnage – Thank you both for being answers to our prayers. We prayed that wherever our daughter went there would be people who loved the Lord that would share God's truth and love with her, and you both did just that. Thank you for being led by the Spirit of God and being bold enough to share the truth of God's Word with our daughter. I love you Tanea and Tanya!

To Beverly Lambert – Thank you for keeping me focused on completing this book, which included, but was not limited to, making checklists, schedules, arranging meetings, researching, etc. Thank you Bev for loving my family and me, and for being willing to help us in any and every way. I love you Bev!

To LeWan Hutchison – Thank you for your heart in wanting to help me with this project. The countless hours that you made yourself available to assist pulling out of me exactly what the book needed to say. I love you LeWan!

To Tanisha Wilcox – Thank you for allowing the book to minister to you and providing edits and feedback that will make this assignment an even greater impact in the lives of those who read this book. I love you Tanisha!

To Anita Smith of ALS Graphics – Thank you for creatively putting on paper what I saw in my head. I love you Anita!

To Camille Dogbe – Thank you for selflessly assisting me throughout the publishing process. I really appreciate you sacrificing your time to help make my book a success. I love you Camille!

To Jonessa Lindsey – Thank you for putting the finishing touches on my book. I appreciate your help. I love you Jonessa!

Foreword

I count it an honor and privilege to write the foreword for my wife's first book, I Want My Daughter Back: A Mother's Journey with God to Free Her Daughter. Writing a book about getting free from homosexuality in the twenty-first century contradicts society's acceptance, media's portrayal, and laws established to promote the lifestyle.

There are even religious leaders who have embraced the lifestyle. The question is, has God changed His mind concerning homosexuality? The answer is 'no'. The Bible says He is the same yesterday, today, and forever (Hebrews 13:8). God loves the homosexual, but hates the act (Leviticus 20:13).

In spite of the controversy, there are many who want to see those they love free from the grips of this ungodly lifestyle. My wife and partner in ministry accepted the challenge. Danielle takes the reader on a journey into our private lives to share the challenges and triumphs we faced with our daughter as she explored homosexuality – the tears, the mistakes, the rebellion, the prayers, the faith in God, the confessions.

Freedom from homosexuality is near and dear to my heart – not just because our daughter was challenged with this, but because your daughter/son, your granddaughter/son, your niece/nephew, your sister/brother, your friend might be challenged with this. The Bible says that we should bear one another's burdens (Galatians 6:2). In this book, Danielle uncovers it all for the sole purpose of turning the attention of the reader to God who guided us through the entire process. He is our hope and our deliverer. Although there is a growing market and acceptance for the homosexual lifestyle, there is great comfort in knowing that God has a way of escape. Our prayer is that by the time you finish reading this book you will have the tools needed to stand in the gap for your loved one.

Timothy McLean

Introduction

The Text Message

It must have been around 10:00 p.m. on May 5, 2012. My husband and I were lying in bed watching television. Two of our three children were asleep in their room and I received a text message from a friend of ours. It was a forwarded text message that my friend had received from someone else. The text went something like, "I don't want to be identified but I heard that Elder Tim and Minister Danielle's daughter is gay. My sons go to the same school that she attends and said that she has 'come out' at school."

After reading the text message, I thought I was going to pass out. I started shaking; I actually became light headed. I do not know if I was still breathing. I felt awful, my mind was racing, and my hands started to sweat. I was trying my hardest to hold on to the phone so that it would not fall out of my hands. I did not want to alert my husband too quickly, because he would have asked too many questions. I just wanted to get out of the room with no questions asked, so I managed to get out of bed without disturbing him.

I walked down the hall and heard my daughter's television still on. I stood in the doorway, but she was asleep. I gently woke her up and said, "I need to read something to you." I proceeded to read the text to her. She denied it over, and over, and over again. This went on for about 20 minutes. I finally said to her, "It will be better for you to tell me the truth because I'm going to find out!" After minutes of probing, she finally confessed and said, "Mom, I'm sorry." She continued by saying that she wanted to tell me, but she was scared and did not know how.

I went back into my bedroom and decided I had no other choice and could not stall this any longer and told my husband. We returned to her room together and the investigation began. My husband asked for her cell phone and she reluctantly gave it to him.

He read all of her text messages. We could not believe the profanity and derogatory language that she was using. He then looked at all of the pictures on her cell phone. The pictures of the young lady on the phone revealed a level of sexuality and sensuality that can be compared to what is seen in Victoria's Secret commercials and magazines. She was in multiple positions that were meant to arouse my daughter. My daughter was only fifteen! How often did my daughter look at these? Was this turning her on? I was mortified. I nearly vomited. I could not believe what I was seeing. Not only was my daughter's innocence being lost, but it was being lost to a young lady and not a male. In this moment, I was dealing with two issues which were in direct violation of my spiritual beliefs and beliefs we had taught our daughter.

My daughter just sat on her bed watching us and answering question after question after question. She was not able to come up with a lie quick enough to answer us, so we kept interrogating her as though we were lawyers and she was a hostile witness. My husband and I were a tag team; he was asking questions and I was asking questions - back and forth. I experienced so many emotions in that short period of time; adrenaline was rushing through my body. I was so hot, and I was so furious that I wanted to punch her in the face and hit her in the stomach. I allowed my daughter to take me to a place in my past where conflicts were handled physically. My daughter was in unchartered territory and had never experienced this side of me. I was angry, ashamed, disappointed, unclear, and distrustful. In the midst of these emotions, I also wanted to hug her and tell her that everything was going to be alright. Strangely, at the same time, I felt sorry for her. She was a lost child who had ventured out in a world for which she was not ready. She reminded me of a puppy who strayed away from the protective covering of its mother. I looked at my husband and he had a look of unbelief on his face. He said to her, "Who are you? Who have you become? How had this happened?" She was speechless. The questioning continued, "Who is this girl? Has she been in our home?" She provided a name and admitted that the other young lady had been to our home. My daughter had also been to her home several times. We had even dropped her off to the young lady's house. Imagine that? There she was, looking totally innocent. Looking at her I would have never thought she was engaged in sexual perversion. Thankfully, the young lady never spent the night at our home, nor did our daughter ever spend the night over her house. They met at the high school my daughter attended during her sophomore year.

Needless to say, my husband and I did not get an ounce of sleep that night. We both cried and just kept asking ourselves, "How did this happen?" We attended church, were in leadership, and worked for the church fulltime - I had Minister in front of my name, and my husband had Elder in front of his. This sort of thing was not supposed to happen to us. But it did. So what do we do now? How do we handle it? The embarrassment. The shame. People whispering about us and our daughter. I am not talking about the people in the world; I am talking about the people in the church. Unfortunately, in some churches, when things happen to children of those in leadership that business is hot off the press. That means people saying, "Did you hear about Elder Tim's and Minister Danielle's child?" We were going to be the topic of the "spit press". So we had some serious decisions to make: Are we going to try to hide this news? Are we going to be totally transparent and not care who finds out? Are we not going to care what they think? So, we went with the latter. We could not go into hiding, and we could not be concerned about who knew what. We put it all out there. This seemed like the longest night ever, and the next morning we told our daughter, "This is your life, and as a result of the decisions you have made, you will have to deal with the consequences."

All night long I went over observations and conversations that I had with her prior to this day. Before this, I had noticed some subtle outward changes. I recall around Easter my daughter wanted to cut her hair shorter and change her typical attire for church. In a picture taken Easter Sunday, myself and a group of young ladies posed for a picture and my daughter was not in a dress. She had on fitted jeans, an oversized blazer, flats, and tapered short haircut. She looked rather metrosexual to me. In this photo, her look was completely different than what was her normal, which was heels, dresses, skirts, and longer more feminine hair styles. I remember asking her if she was having a challenge with her sexuality. The answer was always, "No!" I picked her up every day from school, and I would watch how she interacted with her classmates – it was just a little different. I noticed that her attire changed just a little. She started looking a little more masculine. I noticed how she changed her walk when I was around. She became intentionally softer, more feminine because she knew I was looking. I noticed her boyish posture (a mother notices everything.) When I would ask her about her posture and stance, she always had a good response ready (actually a lie). She would say to me, "Mom, I'm cool at school." Thinking back on this, I believe her being cool, was her way of being accepted and belonging with her peers. Her change in appearance and her sexual identity was now the most important thing in her life. But, I still wondered how she could have thrown out everything she was taught to be "cool", or to belong. Once I found out that my daughter was involved in a homosexual relationship, her being free was most important to me.

I did not write this book to highlight any particular sin. I wrote this book to highlight that we must walk by faith and not by sight concerning every situation, circumstance, or adversity that comes up in our lives or our family's lives. We must believe God and His Word. We cannot give up on what God has promised us. Understanding this, I told God, "I want my daughter back!" This is not what I saw for my kids. They should not be experiencing anything less than God's best in their lives. I refused to give the devil my daughter and accept and believe that this was just a phase in her life. I wanted her innocence restored, so I decided to fight. God spoke Proverbs 11:21 to me, "The seed of the righteous is delivered." I have been standing on this scripture along with other scriptures which I will discuss throughout the book. Hopefully something that you read will assist you with standing in faith if you are believing God for your spouse, your children, your mother, your father, your extended family, or your friends. Do not Give Up! Don't stop believing until you see the manifestation of your prayers! I wrote this book in great anticipation of sharing with you, and taking you through my journey of winning my daughter back.

Chapter One

Was It My Fault?

When this news broke, my husband was an Elder and I was a Minister. I was also on the Board of Directors, the pastoral staff, and a fulltime employee working directly for the pastor and his wife. I worked very hard and enjoyed what I did, had many titles, and had lost the importance of my relationship with the Lord.

Over 12 years ago when I believed God for a job, I told God specifically, "All I want to do is take care of the pastor's wife – just whatever I can do to make her life easier." I remember walking around the parking lot daily praying and thanking God for the job. I did this for over a year, and one day I was offered the position of Personal Assistant to the pastor's wife. I was on cloud nine! God had answered my prayer, and I did whatever she needed: I grocery shopped, I took her children to whatever appointments they had, and I assisted her in ministry in whatever capacity was needed at any time. One of my favorite assignments was going to the mall to pick up or return items for her, and I also loved travelling with her everywhere she ministered which was absolutely awesome.

Some of the most demanding work included assisting with and coordinating women's conferences. But, I did not mind and enjoyed what I did, making sure to give it my all. If that was not enough, I became the Director of Aviation about 7 years later, which was another major responsibility. I managed two pilots, four mechanics, and one airline stewardess. This was no light task, in addition to my responsibilities as the pastor's wife's personal assistant. To manage two aircrafts takes the wisdom of God – especially since I had no prior aviation training or schooling. With God all things are possible, and God made me look good when I had to sit in meetings with experts in this field and hold intelligent and technical conversations. No matter how small or how large the task, I was there to assist. In addition to all of my church responsibilities, I also had a husband and three children. My plate was full and running over, to say the least.

As you can imagine, I did not have much time to spend with God. I was just too busy. I would wake up in the morning and quicklly greet God saying, "Good morning Father, good morning Jesus, good morning Holy Spirit." After all, it would be rude not to speak to Him in the morning. This was engraved in my mind, which I still do to this day. My next step was to get in the shower. This is where I would try to say a quick prayer. You know the one, "This is the day that the Lord has made, let us rejoice and be glad in it. Thank you God, for your protection, provision, and presence, in the name of Jesus. Amen."

Then it hit me. Maybe it was my fault?

Then it hit me. Maybe it was my fault? God was trying to talk to me all along. I was the one that had moved away from sitting down with Him, spending quality time with Him, fellowshipping with Him, and waiting for Him to speak back to me. I stopped singing to Him. I had stopped worshipping Him. I had moved away from His presence and from His Word. I was far away from that feeling that only He could give me. At one time, I longed for His presence. At one time I could not wait to get in His presence and would wake up early in the morning just to be with Him. From salvation until three years prior to this incident, God was my priority. He was everything to me. I talked to Him about all things that concerned me and my life. I included Him in every decision concerning every aspect of my life. However, over the years, with increased responsibilities and increased promotion within my job, I allowed myself to get far away from Him without correcting it – I was caught up in the work of the ministry. I lost my first love. This did not happen overnight; it was gradual. It was day after day after day of not stopping to talk to Him, to hear from Him, to be with Him. This incident with my daughter was an eye opener as to where my relationship with God stood and catapulted me back into His arms.

Working for the church did not get me away from God. That was totally my fault, because my relationship with God is my responsibility. I saw the red flags, but I did not acknowledge them. I remember when I would have to go to the mall for my pastor's wife. The mall was 45 minutes away. God would speak to me and say, "We can talk now while you're riding." Instead, I would call someone and we would talk about other things for the entire ride. I ignored God and denied Him time with me. On the way back, I would talk to someone else. God was no longer my priority. It was like the story of Mary and Martha. Martha was busy working while Mary chose to sit at Jesus' feet and listen to Him. This angered Martha, so she took her frustrations to Jesus. This was His reply:

> "...*Martha, Martha, you are worried and troubled about many things. But one thing is needed, and Mary has chosen that good part, which will not be taken away from her...*" (Luke 10:41-42 (NKJV)).

"That good part" which Mary chose was making Jesus a priority. She had an understanding that regardless of what was going on around her, Jesus was more important. I used to be like Mary, but slowly and subtly had become like Martha. When God would urge me to spend time with Him, I would say to God, "I'm taking care of the pastor and first lady so you and I should be good. God, you see all that I'm doing for them? I'm working hard to make it happen for them." I had convinced myself that everything I was doing was for God. The truth is, God did not have a problem with me working hard for the pastor and first lady. He had a problem with me wanting to please them more than I wanted to please Him. What I failed to realize is that God had placed in me the desire to serve, but it was my job to keep Him at the center. He wants us to be the best at whatever we are doing. He wants us to give our best in whatever we are doing. He has engineered us to be, to do, and to give our best because we have been created in His image and likeness. Unfortunately, my focus had shifted to taking care of my pastor and first lady and not taking care of the most important things that God had given to me – my relationship with Him and my family.

When I received the news about my daughter, I said to myself, "Why didn't I know? Why didn't God show me this? Why was I sucker punched like this?" I had so many questions. On the night we received a text message that shifted my entire world, God instantly became my priority. I had not made time to talk to Him. I cried, was angry, was hurt, felt ashamed, and felt embarrassed. I needed to talk to God. I needed to talk to my Father. I needed to talk to my confidante. I needed to talk to my best friend. Initially, I felt a little awkward when I started praying, because it was almost one of those, "God if you get me out of this one, I will serve you better all the days of my life..." prayers. As I settled down, I knew

I needed to repent. I acknowledged that I had gone off track by not spending time in God's presence, His Word, and relying on Him. As soon as I repented, the weight of it all was lifted. These two scriptures provided peace and comfort:

"If we confess our sins, He is faithful and just to forgive us our sins and to cleanse us from all unrighteousness..." (1 John 1:9 (NKJV))

"There is therefore now no condemnation to those who are in Christ Jesus,[a] who do not walk according to the flesh, but according to the Spirit..." (Romans 8:1 NKJV))

God began speaking to me and correcting me. He told me where I went wrong and showed me the person I had become. I told God, "I'm here about my daughter, not about me". God told me, "It all starts with you." This was a hard conversation with God because I was brought face to face with the woman I had become – the woman who was caught up in the microwave society. The drive-thru society in which praying to God was rushed, quick, repetitious, and no-thought required type of prayer leading to nothing more than superficial time with Him.

Life for Danielle McLean changed that night.

As I lay on the bed crying, I apologized to God for what I had allowed our relationship to become. I knew better. I was sobbing bitterly at the hurt that I caused myself, my family, and God. I had talked to and counseled more than enough people regarding their need to reconnect with God. But, it took this news about my daughter to get my attention about doing the very same thing. Life for Danielle McLean changed that night. I returned that night to my first love. I made some decisions that night to get my relationship back with my God, my father, my best friend, my confidante, my healer, my deliverer, my peace, my everything. I could not get the words out fast enough. I thanked God for never leaving me or forsaking me (Hebrews 13:5). Suddenly, my bitter and sad tears turned into tears of joy. It was bursting in newness, rejuvenation, and freshness. If only the situation that we had to now deal with concerning my daughter could be over as fast as me returning to my first love. But that didn't happen. It required walking by faith and not by sight – minute by minute, day by day.

If you have lost your connection with God and have lost your passion and love for God, you can do as I did and say, "God I apologize for getting away from your presence. I apologize for getting caught up in the work of the ministry, caught up in my job, or [put what has separated you from God] in Jesus Name." God has been so good to us. Even though I drifted away from Him, He still loved me. For that I am thankful.

Time to be Honest With Myself and God...

"Martha, Martha, you are worried and troubled about many things. But one thing is needed, and Mary has chosen that good part, which will not be taken away from her ..." (Luke 10:41-42 (NKJV)).

If we are honest with ourselves, most people can agree that there are times in life when we allow other people, places, and things to take priority over God, just as Martha and I. It is easy to allow distractions to keep us from spending time with God. However, God is calling us to participate in "that good part" where a relationship with Him is developed and strengthened – never to be taken away. God desires a trusting relationship where He is first and the most important one to whom we give our time, attention, and heart. Are there things that you have put before God? What are those areas in your life that you hear the voice of God whispering to you? Is God still your first love? Is God tugging on your heart and asking for your time and attention? If so, are you putting off and pushing Him away? Why? Take this time to reflect and write down the answers to these questions and other thoughts about how you may have neglected time or a relationship with God.

If you have neglected your relationship with God, it can be restored. Just ask for forgiveness and you will be forgiven. *"If we confess our sins, He is faithful and just to forgive us our sins and to cleanse us from all unrighteousness"* (1 John 1:9 NKJV). God is ready to restore you and to bring you to the place where He wants you to be in Him.

Confession

I am made in the image of God and will therefore seek His best in my life. I will not neglect my first love – God. I will take time to know and to listen to the voice of God. Without hesitation, I will follow the leading of God. When I am conflicted, I will choose to partake in that good part which will never be taken away from me. I will seek the wisdom, direction, and love of my Father to consume my life. I am a willing participant in this relationship, and will put God first in my life. I will not allow my job, my family, my failures, or any other distraction to pull my attention away. I choose to abide in the presence of God. I will abide in Him, and He in me. God is now and will always be my first love, in Jesus' name.

Chapter 2

What Do I Do Now?

I had to make a firm decision to stand on God's Word. It seems like standing on the Word would be automatic for someone who has been born again for more than 24 years. However, when this happened with my daughter I was doing my best to recall scriptures. On some days, I felt as though I was at a standstill with everything. There were even times when I almost felt like giving up. When I would open my Bible, I did not know where to start. God, through His faithfulness, would remind me of a scripture that was just right for that time. When my emotions were running high and feelings of giving up emerged, God reminded me of Ephesians 6:13 (NKJV):

> *"Therefore take up the whole armor of God that you may be able to withstand in the evil day, and having done all, to stand."*

I was definitely in an evil day. However, I had to stand. I had to continue to stand until what I believed for manifested. One thing was sure, I have never been one to back down in a fight, and I refused to back down now. I had the true revelation that all of heaven was backing me and quitting or giving up was not an option for me – even though I felt like throwing in the towel at times. I knew that my daughter needed me. She needed me to be the woman of God that I had preached to her about so many times in the past. I would share with my children about believing God for everything. I taught them at early ages that God was their source, not us, and that God could use anybody to get to them what they were believing Him for.

I had to practice what I was preaching for my daughter – I had to do this for her.

During this time, I found out so much about myself. I had the Word hid in my heart, but prior to this incident, it just was not my priority. I could recall the scriptures, but there was no intimacy with it. Ten years prior, I was a serious student of the Word of God. My husband and I were sponges soaking up the Word with regular study time together. I was once told, "As much as you love God's Word is how much you love God. As much as you trust God's Word is how much you trust God." But as we were thrust into this challenge, I was willing to

I wanted my daughter back!

do what I had to do because I wanted my daughter back. I knew that my child needed us like never before. She needed to see the Word of God in action in her parents.

I was accustomed to my kids receiving accolades and compliments on how well they were doing or how beautiful and handsome they were. This situation was only going to bring whispers and condescending looks. This was unchartered territory for me. It forced me to dig deep into myself to pull out what I knew to do, something I had not done in a long time – open up the Word of God to get the answers and direction I needed. Prior to all of this, I opened up my Bible during church, highlighted scriptures, and took notes, but it was all out of routine. My life had not depended on my time in the Word. Now, I was holding myself accountable to my relationship with God. I was determined to keep Him as my priority.

I remember crying out to God saying, "God I need more scriptures to help me with this!" The first scripture God took me to was James 1:5. It says, "If any of you lacks wisdom, let him ask of God, who gives to all liberally and without reproach, and it will be given to him." (NKJV). God told me that I needed HIS wisdom to get through this.

He also reminded me of how Jesus responded to the devil when he was tempted in the wilderness. Matthew 4:1-11 says:

> *"Then Jesus was led up by the spirit into the wilderness to be tempted by the devil. And when He had fasted forty days and forty nights, afterward He was hungry. Now when the tempter came to Him, he said, 'If You are the Son of God, command that these stones become bread.'*

But Jesus answered and said, 'It is written, Man shall not live by bread alone, but by every word that proceeds from the mouth of God.'

Then the devil took Him up into the holy city, set Him on the pinnacle of the temple, and said to Him, 'If You are the Son of God, throw Yourself down. For it is written:

'He shall give His angels charge over you', and,

'In their hands thru shall bear you up, Lest you dash your foot against a stone.'

Jesus said to him, 'It is written again, 'You shall not tempt The Lord your God.'

Again, the devil took Him up on an exceedingly high mountain, and showed Him all the kingdoms of the world and their glory. And he said to Him, 'All these things I will give You if You will fall down and worship me.'

Then Jesus said to him, 'Away with you, Satan! For it is written, 'You shall worship The Lord your God, and Him only you shall serve.'

Then the devil left Him, and behold, angels came and ministered to Him." (NKJV).

God shared with me that I was going to have to do what Jesus did. He fought every negative thought with the Word of God. Every time a thought came that totally went against the Word of God concerning my daughter I was going to have to cast those thoughts down. 2 Corinthians 10:5 (KJV) says:
"Casting down imaginations, and every high thing that exalteth itself against the knowledge of God, and bringing into captivity every thought to the obedience of Christ;..."

I must say that this was difficult for me at times. I was being bombarded with all kinds of thoughts: She isn't going to change. You have lost your daughter! This is your fault! I learned that our minds are where the devil attacks. He throws darts, the devil is a liar. The Bible describes him as the father of lies (John

8:44), so I knew not to believe him. Any thought that does not align with the Word of God is simply a lie.

When you are faced with a trial, circumstance, or any type of adversity, it takes a lot of discipline to tell yourself to stop pondering on thoughts that exalt themselves against the knowledge of God's Word. I had to speak the Word of God OUT LOUD every time I had one of those thoughts. I had to get a grip and not allow what I was thinking to be spoken out of my mouth. Proverbs 18:21(KJV) says:

> *"Death and life are in the power of the tongue: and they that love it shall eat the fruit thereof."*

I had to become a good steward over my mouth. I could only speak life. I constantly meditated on this scripture and trained myself to not speak what I saw. If I found myself saying something negative, I would stop mid-sentence and say, "Let me say it again..." and continue the conversation. I had to stop just letting anything come out of my mouth concerning her.

Early on when people would ask me how she was doing, I would tell the whole story. After a while God started getting on me about it. He would say, "How many times are you going to keep telling that?" My response was, "I'm being transparent. I don't care what people know." But really, I was just trying to get it out before someone told me what they heard about my daughter. I eventually changed my response. When people would ask about her I would say, "She is doing great!" and kept it moving. I had to speak faith concerning her, and this was hard. I knew what I was experiencing: boyish dressing, verbal disrespect, mean disposition, ignored calls, and talking negatively about us to others. I could not

I had to become a good steward over my mouth.

be moved by what I saw. I could not be moved by what I heard. I could not be moved by her attitude towards us. The Bible says in 2 Corinthians 5:7(KJV), *"For we walk by faith and not by sight."*

He told me whenever I saw my daughter to never make any comments about her hair or her clothes. He also said to take a picture with her. This was extremely difficult because anyone who knows me, knows that I like my children to be very neat and orderly. When I would see her most of the time, her hair was a mess and she started dressing pretty much like a boy. To others it seemed fine, but to me it was unacceptable. God shared with me that I wanted her outside to look normal so she would fit in with everybody else. It was almost like I was covering up the real issue instead of dealing with it in public. It was her inside that needed fixing up. He told me that He was working on the inside of her and once her inside got straight, the outside would follow.

Oh, how I love God! He helped us every step of the way with this. His wisdom guided us through. Thank YOU God! I cannot say it enough. If it was not for God leading and guiding me, talking to me, sharing with me, consoling and comforting me, I would not have been able to be effective at assisting my daughter through this. I researched scriptures on homosexuality to ensure that I was praying the Word of God and not on emotion, stayed in God's presence, prayed in the Holy Spirit, and worshipped God through song and dance. This was my daily routine. I also created a vision board at the beginning of 2013, and on it I have a picture of my family with the word "Restoration" beside it. This is what I believed and am still believing God for. I also have Proverbs 11:21 written on the board and hanging in my closet. Every day I look at it, and I say this scripture out of my mouth throughout the day. I also recite the confession below that a dear friend wrote for us:

> *We declare that our daughter is reconciled to the Will of God for her life.*
> *We declare that she is a virtuous woman conforming to moral and ethical principles, moral excellence, and walks upright.*
> *She knows the truth and shall walk in it.*
> *She is our beloved and faithful daughter in the Lord.*
> *Paul said of Timothy, as we say of her: "We are reminded of her sincere faith, which first lived in Grandma Self, Grandma Robertha and lives in her father, mother, sister, and brother." Yes, we are persuaded that this faith lives in her also.*
> *We declare this to be truth. It is the truth that makes her free.*
> *We bind the spirit of shameful lust.*
> *She will not exchange natural sexual relations for unnatural ones.*
> *She will desire the opposite sex as God intends and will remain a virgin even if she chooses to never marry.*
> *We bind the spirit of lying. Her mouth shall speak truth. The spirit of lying is removed from her. It is replaced with truth.*
> *She is no longer a captive to any abominable spirits.*
> *She is loosed from all unnatural sexual desires and the spirit of lying.*

The Spirit of the Lord God is upon me because the Lord has anointed me to bring good news to the afflicted. He has sent me to bind up the brokenhearted, to proclaim liberty to captives and freedom to prisoners.
We walk in love as we go through this challenge with her.
Love is patient. Love is kind. It does not envy. It does not boast. It is not proud. It does not dishonor others. It is not self-seeking. It is not easily angered. It keeps no record of wrongs. Love does not delight in evil but rejoices with the truth. It always protects, always trusts, always hopes, always perseveres.
She is free! It is in the mighty name of Jesus that is done.

In total dependence on God, I was in great anticipation and faith for the manifestation of my daughter's deliverance and the restoration of my family. It was the daily walk with God, reading scriptures, confessing the Word, and obeying the voice of God which allowed me to begin to deal with this test in our lives.

Time to be Honest With Myself and God...

"Casting down imaginations, and every high thing that exalteth itself against the knowledge of God, and bringing into captivity every thought to the obedience of Christ (2 Corinthians 10:5)."

It is safe to say that taming my tongue and my thoughts was not an easy task. However, I had to learn how to control what I was thinking and what I was saying. I had to use the wisdom of God in knowing what to say, when to speak, and how to say things. If you take introspection into your thought life and what you speak, what do you see? Just as I had to bring every thought and word under the authority of God, you must do the same. Take time to reflect on your situation and those areas that you have not cast down to the obedience of Christ. What are you saying that is contrary to the Bible? What thoughts creep into your mind that you have allowed to remain there too long? When a thought or word that is contrary to the Word of God comes, how will you respond? What will be your plan of action when you are challenged to think or speak contrary to God's Word?

_____

_____

_____

_____

_____

_____

_____

_____

_____

_____

_____

_____

_____

Confession

On this day, I will speak only what God says in His Word. I cast down every thought related to [put those areas related to your situation here]. I will no longer allow my mind to wander and think about things contrary to the Word of God. I will think and speak what is true, what is noble, what is just, what is pure, what is lovely, and what is of a good report. I will mediate on the things of God. My thoughts and tongue are aligned with the Word of God. I will speak life that will cause change to occur in my life and the life of others. I will no longer allow my wisdom to be most important, but I yield to the leading and prompting of Holy Spirit. When Holy Spirit reveals the areas in my thought life and speaking that do not align with the Word of God, I will quickly repent and adjust my words and thoughts to be pleasing to God. I will not be unstable when there are situations beyond my control. I will no longer seek my way of handling negative situations and challenges in my life, but will take all things captive to the obedience of Christ in Jesus' name.

Chapter 3

Hearing from God

"He who has an ear, let him hear what the Spirit says to the churches."
(Revelations 2:7a (NKJV))

I am so thankful that I have ears to hear God's voice. Hearing from God is what guided me through this entire process. He gave me (and continues to give me) specific instructions for my life, family, ministry, business, and everything that concerns me. John 10:4 (NKJV) says, *"....and the sheep follow Him, for they know His voice"*. John 10:27 (NKJV) says, *"My sheep hear My voice, and I know them, and they follow Me."* As believers, we have the awesome privilege of hearing God's voice. In the Old Testament, God spoke to His people audibly because they did not have a Bible to use as a guide, nor did they have Holy Spirit living on the inside of them to lead and guide them. They had to depend on God speaking to them audibly. Today, however, we have the Bible and Holy Spirit to guide us. God can speak to us through His Word, other people led by Holy Spirit, and audibly. Believe me when I tell you that I was open to hearing from God in whichever way He saw fit. God spoke to me in the following ways on behalf of my daughter:

His Word

Reading my Bible on a consistent basis is what allowed me to be acquainted with hearing God's voice. I understood that getting my daughter back meant searching and meditating on scriptures that would cause my faith in God to increase causing my daughter to be free from sexual perversion. Here is one of my favorites:

"Behold, I give you the authority to trample on serpents and scorpions, and over all the power of the enemy, and nothing shall by any means hurt you." (Luke 10:19 (NKJV))

This scripture confirmed in me that the devil is and will always remain defeated, and that God has given me authority over the enemy. There were moments when going through this that feelings of inferiority crept in to make me believe that the situation in my life could not change. This scripture made me stand up with boldness and know beyond a shadow of doubt that the devil cannot have anything that I am believing God for. Even still, when I quote this scripture I envision myself keeping the devil under my feet – exactly where he belongs.

Other People

One of the intercessors in our ministry told me that God showed her a vision of my daughter teaching boldly on a stage to a room full of young adults. She said she saw that the room was dark and that a spot light was on my daughter as she was sharing her testimony about how God delivered her from sexual perversion. This brought tears to my eyes because I knew what God had told me concerning my child and what she would do for Him. He continues to remind me of this and never ceases to amaze me. He is faithful to what He has promised, and has confirmed this again through others who have spoken to me concerning my daughter.

Audibly

God has spoken audibly to me several times concerning my daughter. One specific time He told me that when I am in conversations with her, not bring up the bad decisions she made in the past, not even jokingly. This was vital because when I did this in the past, her countenance changed and she would shut down. Love covers and keeps no record of wrong doings (1 Corinthians 13:5 paraphrased). So what did I do? I stopped bringing up her past immediately.

It is not always easy to follow God's instructions. Many times He is telling us to do something that takes us out of our comfort zone. Over the years I have become better at hearing God and following His instructions, but I sometimes missed it still. One day during praise and worship at one of our church services, God spoke to me and said, "Call your daughter up to the front and have her to lead a song". I told God, "Oh no. She might cut up." I totally disobeyed God and felt terrible afterwards. I was more concerned about her behavior than obeying God.

Later that day I asked my daughter if God had said anything to her during service. She responded with, "Yes, He told me to sing." I blew a major instruction. While I convinced myself that she would respond negatively, God had already prepared her. At that moment, I told myself that I would do better at obeying what I hear God telling me to do. For me to know that God is still speaking, gives me so much joy because it shows how much He cares for me and is taking care of my needs. His voice confirms that I do not have to do life on my own. He is with me and is perfecting everything that concerns me (Psalm 138:8).

> *I wanted to hear God so clearly...I would only do what would bring her deliverance.*

As believers, we should know the voice of our God. Too many of us are following other voices; any voice that says anything other than God's Word is that of a stranger. John 10:5 (NKJV) says:

> *"Yet they will by no means follow a stranger, but will flee from him, for they do not know the voice of strangers."*

I wanted to hear God clearly so that I would do only what would bring her deliverance. However, my daughter also had a choice to make that would bring about freedom in her own life. Although I was listening to God and training my ears to hear, I had to pray and continue to believe that my daughter would one day hear from God for herself. Throughout the Bible there are occurrences of men and women hearing the voice of God and then making a choice to obey or disobey. God spoke to Adam in Genesis 2:16-17 (NKJV):

> *"And the Lord God commanded the man, saying, 'Of every tree of the garden you may freely eat; but of the tree of knowledge of good and evil you shall not eat, for in the day that you eat of it you shall surely die'."*

Later in Genesis 2, God made Eve, and in the next chapter the devil comes on the scene talking to Eve about what God said to Adam. Eve should not have had a conversation with the devil; however, as he is questioning her, she adds to what God initially told Adam. Genesis 3:1-5 says:

"Now the serpent was more cunning than any beast of the field which the Lord God had made. And he said to the woman, 'Has God indeed said, You shall not eat of every tree of the garden?' And the woman said to the serpent, 'We may eat the fruit of the trees of the garden: but of the fruit of the tree which is in the midst of the garden, God has said, You shall not eat it, nor shall you touch it, lest you die."

God never said not to touch it, showing that Eve added to God's instructions. Then the serpent said to the woman:

"You will not surely die. For in that day God knows that in the day you eat of it your eyes will be opened and you will be like God, knowing good and evil." (Genesis 3:4-5 (NKJV))

Why is Eve carrying on a conversation with the serpent? Can't you just hear the devil saying, "Come on Eve, don't believe what God said." In the event that you find the devil throwing thoughts in your mind about what God has told you, do not have a conversation with him. Speak the Word of God out of your mouth. This is essential for deliverance and was imperative for me as I was taking this walk of faith concerning my daughter.

This was a real wake up call for me. I had to be honest with myself.

The serpent appealed to the part of Eve that was one of her greatest areas of strength – her intellect and reasoning. Satan chose to attack this area without hesitation. Because I knew the calling on my daughter's life, it was no mystery to Satan that she was my seed. His only goal was to destroy her by any means necessary. At times I wondered what he said to her that allowed her to reason with homosexuality? What did he bring to her mind that gave her a false reward for this behavior? What power did he promise her? Just as Eve thought that she was gaining increased knowledge and power, Satan had to present some reward or gain through this act of homosexuality.

This was a real wake up call for me. I had to not only deal with my daughter's situation, but be honest with myself. What message did I send to my own kids about God? Was I so dedicated to the church and ministry that I misinformed them about who He really is? Why hadn't I listened to God before all of this? I had to look back on my relationship to see where I had fallen short. Unfortunately, my disobedience blinded me to what was happening in my own home.

Just as Eve was blinded by what was forbidden, I too was blinded. Prior to this situation, I was blinded because I had put my relationship with God on the back end of my life. I was more focused on what I enjoyed about my job and pleasing my pastors more than pleasing God. I focused more on less important things than studying the Word and hearing from God. My ears became dull, and my desire for God became secondary.

It was this situation with my daughter that revealed my need to follow God and to hear from Him. The only way Satan's deceptions are revealed is to know the truth of God's Word. I had to get back into the Word and reconcile my relationship with God, so that I could hear Him clearly. Adam and Eve had no idea of how their sin would impact us today. So, I could not allow Satan's voice to impact future generations of my family through this. I had to silence the enemy.

How was I going to silence the enemy? By setting myself to hear from God daily, I would ensure that I was making the right decisions at the right time for my family. Philippians 2:12-13 reassured me that God was working everything out for His good pleasure. This challenge was going to be a catalyst of change for others. Although I had my own thoughts and plan as to how her deliverance would take place, God's plan superseded and ultimately He was going to get the glory out of her life. I made a conscious decision to completely surrender all to God.

Praise and worship was the first thing on my daily agenda, then, spending time reading and confessing the Word followed. Having a 45-minute phone conversation with a girlfriend on the way to the mall was no longer acceptable. I was desperate to hear from God; therefore, I made the necessary adjustments and sacrifices. I was sure not to say or do anything contrary to what God spoke to me or what I read in His Word. I was focused, full of anticipation, and ready to get my daughter back!

Time to be Honest With Myself and God...

"Yet they will by no means follow a stranger, but will flee from him, for they do not know the voice of strangers..." (John 10:5)

When you are faced with challenges, who do you immediately run to? Do you take advice from friends, television personalities, or books you have read? Or do you seek to sit still before God to hear what He has to say? Make a list of those distractions and write down what you believe God is saying to you concerning your situation. Then make a decision to get rid of each distraction and make more time to hear from God. Lastly, consider if God had been speaking to you either through His Word, other people, or in an audible voice that you have ignored. What was He saying to you and how was He trying to speak to you?

_____

_____

_____

_____

_____

_____

_____

_____

_____

_____

_____

_____

If you are not used to hearing the voice of God or have never experienced hearing from God, pray that He will open your heart and ears to be sensitive to His voice. Ask God to show you how to know His voice above all others. Pray, believing that He will speak to you, teach you how to hear from Him, and that you will follow through in obedience to what you hear Him speaking to you.

Confession

I follow only the voice of God – I will not listen to a stranger's voice. My heart and spirit are aligned with the heart and Spirit of God. I see my situation as God sees it and will speak as He speaks. Faith comes as I hear from the Word of God. Every challenge in my life has an answer from God that is revealed to me. I am quick to hear and obey the voice of God. I am so desperate to hear that I remove every distraction and interference that inhibits my ability to hear from my Father. Nothing shall get in the way of my hearing from the one who created me and loves me with an everlasting love. I am sensitive to the voice of God and will allow Him to speak to me as He chooses. Each day I seek the Father, His direction, and His answers to address all challenges I face and am thankful that my ears, heart, and spirit are open to God and receive from Him, in Jesus' name.

Chapter 4

Why Wouldn't She Just Listen?

Growing up, my daughter was strong willed. She was the child who asked 1,001 questions. If she did not like your answer, she would keep asking to try to get you to change your mind. As people say, "She danced to her own beat." She was the child who pushed the envelope for almost everything. I never wanted to break her spirit so I gave her a little more rope than I gave my oldest daughter.

She was, and still is, highly intelligent, beautiful on the inside and out, but what I found out was that she did not think so and felt the need to fit in with others. She was strong in certain areas, but socially she had a need to be liked. As a result, she did whatever it took to belong to certain peer groups. She always compared herself to our oldest daughter and compared our love towards the two of them. We never thought that we treated them differently and always felt like we gave them the same amount of attention. We felt like we treated them both as individuals; yet, her perception was her reality. My daughter is the middle child, and I never bought into the "middle child syndrome." She felt like she received the short end of the stick. She told us that our youngest and oldest got away with everything and that she was blamed for everything. She felt like we singled her out when it came time to correcting them. Again, my husband and I never set out to make her feel this way, but she still felt this way in spite of our intentions.

I am the type of mother who is quick to say, "Get over it and get yourself together!" I am pretty much a no nonsense person, and I do not allow pity parties. I soon learned that this strategy did not work for this particular daughter. She needed me to be more compassionate with her. As a result of her "coming out," she needed more of my time and attention, one-on-one time with me, and to sit down and talk with her so that she could express herself. Hindsight makes me wish I would have stopped and given her what she needed instead of giving her what I thought she needed – a "get yourself together speech". Please remember, during this time I was extremely busy with work and did not have time to cater to her. Let me correct that – I did not make time to cater to my child.

During this discovery of our daughter's involvement in a homosexual relationship, her relationship with me and her father was tried on every level. She refused to listen to us. She continued to be in the relationship with the young lady even after we shared scriptures with her about how this was an abomination to God. She lied to us at every turn. My husband confiscated her cell phone because we were not going to finance her disobedience and rebellion: cursing on her phone, looking at almost nude pictures, and continuing with ungodly behavior.

> *...we must seek God's wisdom for each child in how to discipline them.*

What I also discovered about my daughter was that taking things from her did not stop her, nor did it get her attention. As parents we must seek God's wisdom for each child in how to discipline them – each child is different. After confiscating her cell phone, she began taking our iPads to the bathroom and staying in the bathroom for almost 30 minutes. She would say that she was using the restroom. We thought this was unusual behavior but I wanted to believe her. My husband would tell me what was going on, but I always wanted to give her the benefit of doubt. We eventually found out that when she would go to the bathroom, she was using our iPad to text.

We confronted her and her scheme was busted – so no more taking our iPads in the bathroom. One thing I totally believe is that God will not have us ignorant of the devil's devices (2 Corinthians 2:11). When we approached her about this, there was so much lying. It became so bad that we could not believe a word that came out of her mouth. I remember another occasion where we found out that the young lady had given our daughter an iPod so that they could communicate. We did not know this early on, but we eventually discovered it. One day my daughter told a family friend that she had an iPod. The family friend brought our daughter to us and she confessed to us that she had been using the girl's iPod to communicate.

We felt like we were making progress with her because she was the one coming to us. We returned the iPod. I sincerely believe that our daughter was trying to break it off, but the pressure to remain in the relationship intensified and she was not strong enough to say no. Satan was able to grab hold of her through her teenage rebellion. The subtle messages in the music she was listening to, peer acceptance of alternative lifestyles, and buying into the middle child syndrome all contributed to the stronghold that had her bound. Mark 3:27 (NIV) says:

> "...In fact, no one can enter a strong man's house without first tying him up. Then he can plunder the strong man's house."

I came to the realization that there was a war going on for my daughter's soul. I now had to tie up the strongman that had entered my house. During time in prayer, God told me that homosexuality was not the source and that I needed to get to the root of the problem. He said that the seat of it all was rebellion. I Samuel 15:23a says, *"Rebellion is as sinful as witchcraft and stubbornness as bad as worshiping idols."* (NLT). We could not allow witchcraft in our home. What accompanied this spirit was deception, stubbornness, manipulation, and control. The Word of God is clear in that these things are in direct contrast to who He is and this was not going to be tolerated in our home. We loved our daughter dearly, but we had a responsibility to go after the spirit that had her bound.

Little did we know that the young lady gave the iPod right back to our daughter. Let me take this time to encourage parents to be aware of the electronic devices in your kids' possession – even devices that you may not have purchased. Check everything out – book bags, purses, gym bags, etc. I have definitely come to realize that our children are so technologically savvy. Even the younger children can sometimes run circles around us using different devices and technology. With their knowledge of how to access this information, they know how to delete the data as well. God will show you what is going on with your children – just keep your eyes and ears open, pay attention, and listen to the voice of God. God will show you everything that concerns your life, and Holy Spirit will guide you into all truth – even truth as it relates to your children. As parents, we often dismiss the fact that Satan will aggressively attack our children and use what is in their world to subtly and sensually entice them. If we ignore what is revealed to us by Holy Spirit, we are not only allowing our children to be impacted, but generations after.

In the beginning, I overlooked so much. My husband, on the other hand, recognized what was going on. Anxious to see a change, I started over compensating her by taking her shopping more and trying to keep her busy so she would not have any down time. I felt like keeping her busy was going to keep her away from the young lady and the temptation. Well, that did not work, and I was tired of running around everywhere, spending money, and getting nowhere. I really had to get out of the way. I was trying to fix it in my own ability. Then, I was reminded of Zechariah 4:6b (NKJV): *"Not by power not by might but by My (God's) Spirit..."* I finally accepted that my way was not going to change anything.

> *It was the grace of God and our teamwork that helped us to get through...*

My husband was right there to remind me that *"...the weapons of our warfare are not carnal..."* (2 Corinthians 10:4). There I was, trying to handle a spiritual matter in the natural. I told my husband, "You tell me what to do with her, how to do it, when to do it, and where to do anything concerning our daughter." I knew that I was being led by my flesh, the physical senses: what I saw, heard, touched, smelled, and felt. I was not operating in faith at all. I was consumed with what was happening externally. Initially, I was a mess. I thank God that my husband and I were and still are a team; where I was weak, he was strong. God was faithful in leading and revealing matters to us along the way, and revealing to me how to respond to situations that would bring our daughter closer to her deliverance.

It was the grace of God and our teamwork that helped us to get through what seemed to be a devastating time for us as parents. I mean, we love our kids so deeply and we try to do the very best for them. So naturally it is painful when we see our children going in the wrong direction or worse, being blatantly disrespectful toward us. On more than one occasion my daughter told us that she hated us. Those words hurt us deeply. Through the help of the Holy Spirit we finally arrived to the place where her words stopped having power over us. As we continued to walk by faith and confess the Word of God, we no longer took her words personally. We understood that this was a part of the spiritual battle we were in and had to stay focused on getting her back. This was just a tactic Satan tried to use to derail us from the manifestation of our prayers. She even told us that the young lady said, "Why don't your parents just get over it? We love each other and we are going to be together." I responded by saying, "We will never accept that lifestyle in our home. We love you, but we hate the sin that you are operating in." I had to explain to her that even if this were a boy that she was sexually involved with, we would have the same response. Sin is sin. Homosexuality is not a greater sin than sex before marriage, murder, cheating, or lying.

We tried to do everything to get her out of that environment. We transferred her to another school because we learned that she had classes with the young lady. She had not made a decision to change internally, so all of what was inside of her poured out into everything she said and did. No matter what we wanted for her, if she was not ready to change, she was not going to. With all of our attempts, she continued to be in the relationship with the young lady while attending the new school.

She was convinced that this was what she wanted to do. I remember assisting her with getting a babysitting job. She is very good with children and knows how to get into their world – kids really enjoy being around her. One day I agreed to pick her and the kids up and take them on an outing. When I arrived, we loaded all the children in our truck.

Everyone was excited about the outing, including me. I do not quite remember how it all came out, but one of the children asked my daughter for her iPod. Looking puzzled and confused I asked, "What iPod?" My daughter denied everything. She repeatedly denied having the iPod while giving the little kids a stern look daring them not to go against her lie. Thank God for little children who are so innocent and honest. As she was denying and lying, all of the children kept saying, "You do have an iPod! It's black." Her last denial was more than I could handle at that moment. I remembered that we had prohibited her from having any electronic device, so this really should not have been a topic of conversation. However, it was and I immediately concluded that this device must have come from the young lady, yet again. I lost it right in front of the kids! I was yelling at her for at least 5 minutes without letting up; I was sweating and angry while driving the kids back to their house. When we arrived, I demanded that she go in the house and retrieve the iPod.

Sin is sin.

As we entered the house, I asked her one last time for the iPod and she said she did not have it. I could not handle any more – I exploded and hit her. I was outdone! Thank God I am not a cursing Christian because I probably would have cursed her out. She kept saying, "Mom, I don't have an iPod." Then she relented and told me that the iPod was at our house. So I said, "Ok, let's go to our house because I am determined to get the iPod." On the way, I called my husband and gave him a heads up. When we arrived, he met us at the door and I allowed the children to go outside to play basketball. We both began demanding that she give us the iPod, but she refused.

My husband had a belt and told her, "If you don't give us the iPod, I am going to whip you." She still refused to give it to us. So my husband kept giving her lashes. I know some of you cannot believe this, but the Bible says in Proverbs 13:24 that if we spare the rod, then we hate our child. My daughter, at 16 years old, had not had a spanking since she was about 6 years old, and here she was getting spanked. I hated this, but she refused to listen to us. My husband and I both demanded repeatedly that she give us the device. I do not know if she was exasperated or sore, but she finally gave in and said that it was upstairs in her room. I went searching for the iPod. My husband told her, "If your mother doesn't find it, I am going to continue whipping your tail!" All of a sudden, she ran out the house. She did not even have on shoes! My husband yelled to me saying, "She ran out of the house!" We could not believe this! Needless to say, the iPod was not in her room. We found out later that it was in her sock that she had on.

Now she was a runaway. She ran into the home of someone in the neighborhood. We did not even know the people. I kept ringing the doorbell, but to no avail. Finally, someone answered the intercom and said that my daughter would be out soon. I stood on their front porch for about 30 minutes waiting. In the meantime, my husband called one of his police officer friends who advised him to call the local authorities so that everything could be documented. So that is what he did.

I decided to go back to our house to check on the children who were playing still. I did my best to keep them calm – assuring them that everything was fine, and I was still going to take them out. While I was doing that, my daughter ran out of the neighbor's home and started running through the neighborhood a second time. After she tired herself from running, we saw her walking down the street. My husband took the car, pulled beside her, and told her to get in the car, but she refused and took off running again. The police showed up and we told them everything that transpired. The officer informed us they were acquainted with this type of incident with teenagers. We were exhausted and distraught because we were not familiar with this behavior. Here we were, church leaders, visible to the congregation – was there anyone who attended our church that did not know us, even if it was in name only? Probably not. The good elder and minister's daughter had run away from home. This was totally unbelievable to me – it was like living in a nightmare. How could this be happening to us?

I was shaking all over. The tears could not come out because I was so angry that this foolishness was occurring in my home with my child. There were thousands of questions going through my mind. Even in the midst of all of this, while standing outside, my husband and I came together in prayer. We just held each other and spoke the Word of God to each other. We asked God to protect our daughter while she was out there. We asked Him to put the right people in her path who would minister Jesus to her.

Never in my imagination would I have ever thought that we would be dealing with this. I had previous conversations with my children about these types of things, and I can recall them both saying things like they would never run away.

...the same way she ran away would be the same way that she would run back.

She stayed away for about a week, and we did not go looking for her. I told my husband, as well as others, that the same way she ran away would be the same way that she would run back.

A parent of one of my daughter's friends called me. She could not believe that we were not out looking for our daughter. She even asked me if we loved our daughter because we were not searching all the homes of her friends. It took everything in me to maintain my salvation and respond properly. I explained to her that our daughter would not control our home. Her running away would not make us accept the lifestyle that she was attempting to live nor would it cause us to compromise our standards. I reiterated that we loved our daughter beyond words, but she would not control our home. 1 Samuel 15:23a says:

> *"For rebellion is as the sin of witchcraft, and stubbornness is as iniquity and idolatry. Because thou has rejected the word of the Lord, He hath also rejected thee from being king."* (KJV).

This is exactly what we were dealing with – a rebellious child. Rebellion is:

"...an act against established order and authority. It can be defiance against God's will or resistance to leadership He has ordained. When we insist on doing things our way, we reveal our pride and selfishness."

It was as if we did not even know our own child. She had become a stranger in our home. She did not want to have a conversation with us. She did not want anything to do with us, and this hurt badly. When she was a little girl, she was the child who was my "hip baby." Everywhere I went, she was there with me. We were always together. I attended all of her basketball and volleyball games. Although she was kind of a loner amongst her peers, she was comfortable with being with mommy at home, the grocery store, wherever. She longed for my affection. She was the child who, when next to me, I could feel her breathing. This challenge with my daughter made me feel as though I could not reach her. My heart was heavy most days, but I would remind myself of Isaiah 61:3 (Amplified):

> *"To grant [consolation and joy] to those who mourn in Zion – to give them an ornament (a garland or diadem) of beauty instead of ashes, the oil of joy instead of mourning, the garment [expressive] of praise instead of a heavy, burdened, and failing spirit – that they may be called oaks of righteousness [lofty, strong, and magnificent, distinguished for uprightness, justice, and right standing with God], the planting of the Lord, that He may be glorified."*

I had to put on the garment of praise to get rid of the spirit of heaviness that was trying to consume me. There were days that I would make myself dance around the house and sing praises to God. I had to shout for joy (Psalms 5:11). I simply refused to be sad. My sister would call me and ask how I was doing with all of this and my constant response was, *"The joy of the Lord is my strength"* (Nehemiah 8:10). During this challenge, we had to keep the Word of God on the forefront of our thinking. We saturated ourselves in the Word and God comforted us. We rested in Him and praised Him daily. God said that He inhabits the praises of His people. In other words, He lies down and takes up residency in the place where people praise Him. We did the Word even when it appeared that she was refusing to listen. When operating in faith you cannot be moved by any external facts. Although she was not listening to us, we were assured that God heard and was answering our prayers.

Time to be Honest With Myself and God...

"Not by might nor by power, but by My Spirit..." (Zechariah 4:6b)

As parents we are tasked with the responsibility of raising responsible, wise, God-fearing children. Even with our best, we can fall short and make mistakes, even as I did with my own daughter. While there are times we make mistakes, there are many more times when we are following what God expects, and our children do not want to listen to wise counsel and accept correction. This can lead to poor decisions and turmoil. Unfortunately, when it seems that our children are going down the wrong path, we are tempted to take matters into our own hands. In what ways do you see your children ignoring Godly wisdom and displaying disobedience? Also note below the areas where you have been trying to save your children and doing the work of God. What are the areas that you see are going to require more prayer and yielding to God to handle the matter? Then declare that you will trust Holy Spirit instead of your own power and might.

_____

_____

_____

_____

_____

_____

_____

_____

_____

_____

_____

_____

_____

_____

Confession

I will not get in the way of God working in the life (lives) of my child(ren). [place the name(s) of your child(ren) here] operates in the wisdom, knowledge, and revelation of God. [place the name(s) of your child(ren) here] understands complicated matters and makes good decisions. I will not hinder the work of Holy Spirit in the life of my child(ren). The ears of [place the name(s) of your child(ren)] is(are) sensitive, know(s) your voice, and will not obey the voice of a stranger. I yield to the completed work you have accomplished in the life (lives) of my child(ren) with faith. I am a living example of the love of Christ and will pour that out into my home and into the life (lives) of my child(ren). If I have made a mistake, I am quick to correct it. I am quick to hear and slow to speak when dealing with [place the name of your child(ren) here]. I operate in the spirit of love, joy, peace, longsuffering, gentleness, goodness, faith, meekness, and self-control. I show love that does not keep record, is patient, absent of fear, and selfless. I quickly listen to and obey the voice of God when He directs me to speak to, show action towards, or correct my child(ren). During times of challenge, I will see as God sees, speak His Word, and maintain my posture of faith regardless of what I see before me. I will allow the Spirit of God to move as He chooses to bring victory into our lives in Jesus' name.

Chapter 5

Why Couldn't I Change Her?

Like most Christian parents, I thought if I talked to my daughter and explained to her how what she was participating in was an abomination to God, she would understand, repent, and end the relationship. I shared scriptures with her such as Leviticus 20:13 (NKJV) which says:

> *"If a man lies with a male as he lies with a woman, both of them have committed an abomination. They shall surely be put to death. Their blood shall be upon them."*

None of the scriptures seemed to matter to her. This actually seemed to have the opposite effect; she tried to get the scriptures to line up with what she wanted to do. She would misconstrue the scriptures and confused God's love for her with Him accepting her homosexuality. I had to really walk in love when dealing with my daughter. I had to do what 1 Corinthians 13:4 says: be kind, patient, not irritable or touchy, do not hold grudges, hardly even notice when others do it wrong, loyal to Him no matter what the cost, always expect the best of Him, and always stand your ground in defending. I wanted to yell and scream at her and let her have it, but was constantly reminded of the scripture,

> *"...God's kindness is meant to lead you to repentance..."* (Romans 2:4, ESV)

We had to show how the love of God was shed abroad in our hearts (Romans 5:5). I had to humble myself and speak in a loving tone with her – the total opposite of what I was feeling. My calm interactions with her were so important because I had to keep an open line of communication with her. I did not want to lose her, and more importantly God did not want her lost. Because she often felt as if we did not love her as we did our other children, it was very important to me that I showed her that I loved her and did not hate her. My husband and I loved her dearly and had to act like God. We actually had to be Jesus to her. We had to be Christ-like and demonstrate God's love to her even though we hated what she was accepting as her lifestyle.

As believers, we have been equipped to love people unconditionally through the power of the Holy Spirit. This is how God responds to us. He loves us unconditionally, not because of anything we have done, but loves us in spite of ourselves. Every day I prayed for God to give me wisdom concerning my daughter. I asked God to tell me what to say to her, how to say it to her, when to say it, and where to say it to her. James 1:5 (KJV) says:

> *"If any of you lack wisdom, let him ask of God, that giveth to all men liberally and upbraideth not; and it shall be given him."*

I needed God's wisdom constantly and continuously because my flesh was always ready to say or do something totally outside of the Will of God. In life I have found that people find it easy to come and share with me whatever they are going through. We would talk and I would give them advice or a plan of action, and they would do it. More often, they came back with praise reports – especially those who did precisely what we discussed. What was so frustrating and painful all at the same time was that while I could give others advice and plans of action, I could not get my own daughter to change. I tried everything to get her to change – both naturally and spiritually. After doing this over and over without the results I desired, it hit me. It is not my job to change my daughter. I could not change her. She had to want to change on her own. The more I tried to change her, the more determined she was not to change. She became defiant and started saying, "I was born this way. I'm not going to change. You are just going to have to accept me for who I am."

This was tough for me because it meant that I had to totally walk by faith for her. Faith should be a way of life for believers, but I have found that many believers, including myself, try to make things happen. For many Christians, if things do not happen when we feel like they should, we step right in and assist God. Instead of making things happen, we actually make things more difficult for ourselves and God. Yes, the Bible does say that *"faith without works is dead"* (James 2:26). However, this scripture does not mean that we are to try to change people. We cannot change people! God has given every one of us our own free will. This means that we do exactly what we want to do. It also means what we do not want to do, we will not do.

If faith without works is dead, then faith with works is alive. In my situation, the "work" was simply hearing from God and doing exactly what he told me to do concerning her. He told me to love her unconditionally, to treat her with respect, to welcome her, to not make smart remarks about her outer appearance, to not judge her, and to be nice to her.

We cannot change people!

Yes, be nice. How refreshing. God wanted me to be kind to my daughter, no matter what I saw or heard from her. Talking to her disrespectfully, not demonstrating God's love towards her, alienating her from our family, and referring to her as anything other than a woman of God, means that I am not working the Word of God.

One Sunday morning at church my husband was ministering, and God reminded me of how I stood on His Word for my husband. When we got married, we were very young and neither of us was a born again believer. We both had attended church, but we had never accepted Jesus as our Lord and Savior. Needless to say, we experienced a lot of challenges during the early days of our marriage. It was so bad that I had nowhere else to go, except to the Lord. A friend had told me the scripture to quote when I was ready. One day things got so bad that I pulled out my Bible and quoted out loud Romans 10:9-10.

I expected my husband to automatically change after that; however, that automatic change did not happen. As a matter of fact, things grew much worse before getting better. But, I stood on God's word. I refused to allow the devil to have my husband or my marriage. As my husband was ministering, God told me, *"The same way you believed me for your husband, believe me for your daughter."* God spoke to me so clearly. That was a defining moment for me because I knew how I stood on God's Word for my husband and my marriage. I am still living in the fruit of my prayers for him. I am so glad that I stood on God's Word and did not quit, give up, cave in, or stop believing. In fact, I am still confessing the Word of God over my marriage and my husband. I am still walking by faith concerning this. Faith never stops – it is what every Christian is to live by. I am forever grateful that I have God and that He is with me; He spoke to me clearly

40

that day and I was even more strengthened and encouraged to keep fighting and moving forward in faith.

For my husband and I, we wanted our daughter delivered from homosexuality and restored to our family. What is it that you want back? Is it your spouse, your child(ren), your job, your peace, your joy? What is it? When you have answered that question and know what you want restored, then it is time to take it back! Regardless of what your situation is, regardless of how bad it is, or regardless of how much the devil has tried to tell you that you are the only one going through whatever you are going through, you must walk by faith. Do not allow the devil to convince you that your situation will not change. Remember, he is a liar (John 8:44). Evaluate where you are in life right now. Then dig into the Word of God and put a demand on what it is that you want back. Joel 2:25 (KJV) says:

> *"And I will restore to you the years that the locust hath eaten, the cankerworm, and the caterpillar, and the palmerworm, my great army which I sent among you."*

Stand on God's Word and see everything you are believing for returned back to you. It is not up to you to change anything; it is up to God. Just as I could not change my daughter, I had to use His Word, pray, and believe. I had to trust that my faith in God would produce the restoration I longed for in my family. If I could change her, I would be able to take the credit for it all. God wants all glory to go to Him and will allow situations to happen and then be resolved where we have no other truth except that it was God – which gives Him all of the glory.

Time to be Honest With Myself and God...

"Now hope does not disappoint, because the love of God has been poured out in our hearts by the Holy Spirit who was given to us..." (Romans 5:5)

The most difficult part of manifestation of our prayers is the stage of waiting patiently. I so desperately wanted things fixed and over with when it came to this challenge with my daughter. However, I had to walk in faith and patience to receive the promise. How we wait is just as important as the time we use in waiting. During the time of waiting patiently on God to manifest your prayers, what behaviors have you been displaying which are assisting or hindering your breakthrough? In the space below, list what you are believing God for and a corresponding, faith-based action to accompany each item. While you are listing these, pray and ask God to show you how to respond in faith if you are unsure of a proper, Godly response. Remember that with God, all things are possible (Mark 9:23), so do not lose heart in waiting.

_____

_____

_____

_____

_____

_____

_____

_____

_____

_____

_____

_____

_____

Confession

With God, all things are possible. I operate in faith and do not waver. I am not double-minded and only display Godly, faith-based, consistent behaviors to support the manifestation of my prayers. I show the love of God through my actions and words. I speak only what the Word of God says and operate in the wisdom of God, following His direction for every situation in my life. I speak the truth in love and do not manipulate situations and feelings in order to get my way. I hunger and thirst for the Word of God and study the Bible consistently. I believe that when I pray, it has been answered. I readily receive correction when I need it without resentment and in love. Satan is a liar, and I am not fooled nor do I fall prey to any of his schemes and devices. I agree with the timing of God to manifest all things in His divine time and will be anxious for nothing. All glory goes to God! I yield to Holy Spirit to fully restore all that has been lost, in Jesus' name.

Chapter 6

God, When Will This Be Over?

This was a question I asked myself over and over again. I refused to accept that this was the end for my daughter. I knew what God had spoken to me concerning the impact she would make in the Body of Christ. Yet everything that I saw with my eyes did not line up with what God told me. The words that I heard coming out of her mouth did not line up with what God had told me. God told me that my daughter would lead people into His presence with her voice. I was consumed with being led by my senses. She did not look or sound like what I was praying. It was hard for me to turn off my natural senses and turn on my spiritual senses. I was overwhelmed physically, emotionally, and psychologically. The Bible clearly says in 2 Corinthians 5:7 that we walk by faith and not by sight.

I had to stop myself from meditating on the thoughts that she was not going to change. I had to stop myself from curling up in a ball and constantly seeing images of my daughter involved in sexual acts. My mind was being bombarded with thoughts and images that totally went against God's will for her life. In these moments of weakness, I remember God reminding me of 2 Corinthians 10:5 (KJV):

> *"Casting down imaginations, and every high thing that exalteth itself against the knowledge of God, and bringing into captivity every thought to the obedience of Christ;..."*

I had to do exactly what this scripture said; I had to cast down every thought and every imagination. God was not going to do it for me. I had to do it. The devil likes to throw darts, better known as thoughts, at our minds to get us to doubt

God. When negative thoughts or images come, cast them down and speak the Word of God out of your mouth. It is not enough to just think about the scripture. You have to literally speak it out of your mouth.

I knew what God had spoken to me concerning the impact she would make...

Whatever you are facing, the answer is in the Word of the Living God. God has equipped us to handle every satanic attack. He has thought the whole thing through. Ephesians 6:10-20 (KJV) says:

> *"Finally my brethren, be strong in The Lord and in the power of His might. Put on the whole armor of God that you may be able to stand against the wiles of the devil. For we do not wrestle against flesh and blood, but against principalities, against powers, against the rulers of the darkness of this age, against spiritual hosts of wickedness in the heavenly places. Therefore, take up the whole armor of God, that you may be able to withstand in the evil day, and having done all, to stand. Stand therefore, having girded your waist with truth, having put on the breastplate of righteousness, and having shod your feet with the preparation of the gospel of peace; above all, taking the shield of faith with which you will be able to quench all the fiery darts of the wicked one. And take the helmet of salvation, and the sword of the Spirit, which is the word of God; praying always with all prayer and supplication in the Spirit, being watchful to this end with all perseverance and supplication for all the saints and for me, that utterance may be given to me, that I may open my mouth boldly to make known the mystery of the gospel, for which I am an ambassador in chains; that in it I may speak boldly, as I ought to speak.*

There are two words which are important to clarify: "wiles" and "darts." "Wiles" is defined as "…devious or cunning stratagems employed in manipulating or persuading someone to do what one wants…" God has given you His armor so that you can stand against the devil's strategies. That is great news! You have been empowered by God! He has equipped you so you do not have to accept anything from the devil. Stop allowing the devil to run rampant in your life, in your marriage, in your singleness, in your children's lives, in your ministries, and at your work place. Put on the whole armor of God – not some, but every last part of it and KEEP it on!

> *I had to constantly remind myself of the real enemy.*

"Darts " is defined as "...of strong suggestions and fierce temptations to evil." Concerning the darts, the scripture says, "...above all, take the shield of faith with which we shall be able to quench the fiery darts of the wicked one." The Bible doesn't say, "You may be able to" or "there is a possibility". It says you will be able to. That is a strong statement.

> *"...For we do not wrestle against flesh and blood, but against principalities, against powers, against the rulers of the darkness of this age, against spiritual hosts of wickedness in heavenly places."*

When dealing with my daughter, I had to constantly remind myself of the real enemy and where to put my energy in this fight. I did not pass every test. Sometimes I would say unnecessary things to her in hopes that she would see how ridiculous her decision was. But, when I reflected and really started handling this situation the way God would have me to, this scripture kept me from attacking her or saying the wrong thing to her. Paul, the writer of Ephesians, begins verse 10 with:

> *"Finally, my brethren, be strong in The Lord and in the power of His might"* (KJV).

It sounds to me like he knows this personally to be true. This too became revelation to me. At the time of this writing, my armor is still on. Putting on the full armor of God is daily, not just in tough times, but it must be worn at all times. I had to make a conscious decision throughout each day to keep my mind stayed on Him. Isaiah 26:3 says that God will keep me in perfect peace, if my mind is stayed on him.

For each thought I had to ask myself, "Is this thought from God?", "Is this from me?", or "Is it from the devil?" I stopped allowing my mind to just think on anything. I became focused in my thinking. Philippians 4:8 (NKJV) says:

> *"Finally brethren, whatever things are true, whatever things are noble, whatever things are just, whatever things are pure, whatever things are lovely, whatever things are of good report, if there is any virtue and if there is anything praiseworthy – meditate on these things."*

This scripture is so simple – almost too simple to believe. Right now I want you to take inventory of your thought life. What have you been thinking about in abundance? Does it line up with Philippians 4:8? If so, that is great; if not, you have work to do. The Bible is clear and precise. It says to *"bring EVERY thought..."* Not some of them, but every last thought to the obedience of Christ (paraphrased). No one can do this for you. You have to be purposeful and deliberate in your thinking. Think on the Word of God. Meditate on it day and night. Joshua 1:8 (NKJV) it says:

> *"This Book of the Law shall not depart from your mouth, but you shall meditate in it day and night, that you may observe to do according to all that is written in it. For then you will make your way prosperous, and then you will have good success."*

Again, it is up to you, and you can start right now. Get your Bible and research answers to whatever you are dealing with. If you are dealing with unforgiveness, find all the scriptures you can on love. Write them down and post them all around you. Have scriptures on your bathroom mirror, taped to your steering wheel, on your computer, etc. You must be surrounded by the Word of God in order for the Word of God to be a part of you. What is in you will come out, and there is no other way to have the Word of God to come out unless you put it inside your heart. We must be people who stand on God's Word. Whatever the challenge, you must walk by faith and not by sight. Do not be moved by what you see or do not see – simply believe.

My flesh wanted immediate gratification. It was not that I did not believe God could deliver my daughter or set her free. I just did not want to endure the process of praying and waiting for the manifestation of what I had prayed. I just wanted it over with quickly with every fiber of my being. This was a situation that I could not fix, and I had to totally trust God. All I had was God and His response to things. I had to feast on the fruit of the spirit in order to make it through this. Galatians 5:22 (NKJV) says:

> *"But the fruit of the Spirit is love, joy, peace, long suffering, kindness, goodness, faithfulness, gentleness, self-control. Against such there is no law."*

It is during these times that you really are able to see what you are made of. It is easy to quote scriptures when everything is going well. It is when we feel like our world is falling apart, when we feel like we are in it by ourselves, or just do not know what else to do that panic begins to set in. Believers have to flip this around and be convinced like never before that God's Word is true and that He is faithful to His Word. I did not want my daughter to continue in anything that was outside of the will of God. I also knew that we could not tolerate this spirit running, ruling, or trying to dictate to us in our home. My husband and I came together consistently in prayer. Matthew 18:19 (NKJV) says:

> "Again I say unto you, that if two of you shall agree on earth as touching anything that they shall ask, it shall be done for them of my Father which is in heaven."

Not only did we stand on this scripture, we put God in remembrance of His Word. I had to do what I told so many people in times past, "Stand on the Word of God without wavering!" I could not say what I was seeing, but only speak what I was believing God for in this situation with my daughter. I was determined to do this for as long as I needed to. Her freedom was that important to me. What about you? Are you determined? If so, stand on the Word of God until manifestation.

Time to be Honest With Myself and God...

"Finally, my brethren, be strong in The Lord and in the power of His might..."(Ephesians 6:10).

As you have read, I had to surround myself with the Word of God and allow the power of God to change our situation, not my own intelligence and understanding. What are the areas in your life where you are challenged at this moment? Do you know what the Bible says specifically concerning these areas in your life? Take time to list these areas below. Next, search the Bible and find a scripture that provides an answer for each. Now, it is a daily act of faith to walk out these scriptures in your life. Take time to memorize and post these words around your home, workplace, car, phone, etc. You must walk by faith and not by sight. Satan is your enemy and will do his job to fight against the Word and power of God, but you also have a job. It is your task to speak, apply, and believe the Word of God for every situation you are facing. It is also your job to put on the full armor of God (Ephesians 6:10-20) and to mediate on His Word daily (Joshua 1:8). You are an overcomer!

_____

_____

_____

_____

_____

_____

_____

_____

_____

_____

_____

_____

Confession

I am more than a conqueror in Jesus Christ. I am strong in the power and might of God. I put on the full amour of God and am able to withstand the schemes and wicked devices of Satan. I speak boldly and in faith according to the Word of God. I mediate on the Word of God day and night and do not allow it to depart from my mouth. I weigh every thought against the Word of God, and everything that attempts to exalt itself above the knowledge and power of God, I cast it down. I fight the good fight. I see with my spiritual eyes and do not focus on what I see in the natural. I am strong and a mighty warrior in the kingdom of God. I will not give up and will use the wisdom of God in every situation of my life. I will not lean to my own understanding, but will follow the leading of Holy Spirit. I am armed with truth, righteousness, faith, salvation, the Word of God, and prayer. I will use my spiritual weapons against the kingdom of darkness and will continue to stand through the power and strength of Christ, in the name of Jesus!

Chapter 7

I Got My Daughter Back!

I longed for the day to see with my own physical eyes my daughter's true freedom from sexual perversion. I would daydream about it. I would sit and imagine the relief in our hearts and was in great expectation of this day. When this day came I could take a deep breath and relax. I kept asking myself thought provoking questions: "What did true freedom from sexual perversion look like?" Was it her dressing girly and looking very feminine? Was it her feet pointing straight with painted toes in high heels? Was it her sitting up straight in a chair? Was it her having her hands raised in church? Was it her telling me that she was totally free? I did not know what to look for because in times past she had displayed all of those outward things. She would dress up really pretty. When I was looking, she would point her toes and sit up straight in chairs. She would raise her hands during church service. She would even tell me that she was done with the lifestyle, yet I would later find out she was still bound. She looked the part for me. She knew how to look exactly like what I wanted and even knew what to say to make me think she was free.

Over the years I learned that people can dress up sin, mask sin, and act sinless, but not be free at all. I have watched people come to church Sunday after Sunday, smoke cigarettes and try to cover it up by chewing gum or by putting mints in their mouths as well as putting on perfume. It is amazing what we will do to cover up sin from people. Why are we "people conscience" and not "God conscience"? There is no covering or hiding from God. He is not concerned with the external. He is concerned about our hearts – the internal. 1 Samuel 16:7 (NKJV) says:

"...for the Lord sees not as man sees; man looks on the outward appearance, but the Lord looks on the heart."

Some people are still drinking alcohol, sleeping with people they are not married to, or committing many other sins. Some will lie so fast that it will make your head spin. Some hate other people while some will slander someone's name to the point where others will stop talking to them or end friendships. And yet some are still abusing their wives physically, will still curse out anybody, will cheat on their income taxes, will participate in homosexual practices, or will

I longed for the day to see with my own physical eyes my daughter's true freedom from sexual perversion.

watch pornography like it is daytime television. We see these people every day and think they are free and totally committed to the Word of God, because of what is on the outside. We as believers have to stop lying to ourselves and come clean with what we are dealing with. We have to look deep in our hearts and be honest about what we know about ourselves. This is for believers who really want to stop operating in sin. I have found that some believers have become complacent with the sin that is in their lives.

Through this situation with my daughter, I found that I had moved away from my personal relationship from God. I was wearing a mask and playing the part at church, and God was not my priority. God was speaking to me, but I was not listening because to me, life was good. My children were good. My marriage was good. I was a church leader making decisions and making things happen which were impacting thousands of people. At the same time, I was being deceived. This was a pseudo comfort. God spoke to me and tried to warn me, but I did not listen. Because of my status in the church and how others saw me, I was looked at as being spiritual and well-balanced with seemingly no problems. However, the devil had stepped right in my home and attempted to take over.

My very own daughter did not want to stop her sin – she enjoyed it. But somewhere deep inside of her, she knew it was unacceptable in the eyesight of God. We shared with her 1 John 1:9:

"If we confess our sins, He is faithful and just to forgive us our sins and to cleanse us from all unrighteousness." (KJV)

Being forgiven and cleansed by God begins with our confession. We begin the process by what we say out of our mouths. In John 10:10 Jesus says:

> *"The thief cometh not, but for to steal, and to kill, and to destroy: I am come that they might have life, and that they might have it more abundantly."* (KJV)

Who is the thief? The thief is the devil and his job description is to steal, kill, and destroy any and everything of believers. He wants to kill believers and to steal your testimony, your peace, and your joy. Every promise that God has given us, the devil wants to steal. He wants to destroy our lives and make a mockery out of those who call themselves children of the Most High God. In 1 Peter 5:8 it tells us:

> *"Be sober, be vigilant: because your adversary the devil, as a roaring lion, walketh about, seeking whom he may devour."* (KJV)

The devil does not know who he can devour. The scripture says the devil is walking about "seeking whom he may devour." He is not all-knowing. He is not God – only God is all knowing. We must be sober, vigilant, alert, and aware at all times. I kept asking God, "When God, When?" When I would ask this concerning my daughter, God reminded of what He told me, "I answered that prayer the first time you prayed and asked me to deliver her." He just needed me to stand in faith and believe.

What is funny is that I am sure that God is saying to a lot of us "When [put your name here] When?" When will you truly believe that He heard you the first time? When will you totally rest in knowing that God has already worked out everything that concerns you? Daniel 10:12 shares how God heard Daniel the first time he prayed, but the angel of Persia held up the manifestation of his prayer for 21 days. Rest assured that God heard you the first time. Do not waver. You have no idea what may be holding up that angel, or what fight that angel has to conduct to bring your miracle. James 1:6-8 says:

> *"But let him ask in faith, nothing wavering. For he that wavereth is like a wave of the sea driven with the wind and tossed. For let not that man think that he shall receive anything of the Lord. A double minded man is unstable is all of his ways."* (KJV)

My daughter has made some serious decisions over the past 2 years. I have watched her blossom into the woman of God that He created her to be. I recall one conversation we had recently. I asked her if she ever imagined that her life would be like it was. She emphatically answered, "No! I wouldn't wish the last couple of years on anyone." She then apologized for everything. We sat in our kitchen and tears welled up in my eyes because I was talking to a free woman.

On another occasion, she sent me a text while away at college and asked me what I thought about her getting a nose ring. In response, I posed this question to her: "With the direction you are going and the career path that you are seeking, do you think a nose piercing would be presentable?" What makes this so amazing is that my once rebellious daughter was now asking my opinion. To God be all the Glory! A few days later I texted my daughter to tell her that someone wanted her bank account information so that they could put money in her account monthly. She was very excited. What excited me was what her first comment was. She said, "God is rewarding me for obeying Him". She went on to explain that her friends had just left to go get tattoos and piercings, but that she had decided to not go. This was a major decision, a change for her, and music to my ears. It is one thing for me to know that God is with me, but it is a greater blessing to know that He is with my child and so faithful to all of His promises.

My daughter is now a part of our praise and worship team at our church. She came to me one Sunday and said, "I'm ready to join the team." My husband and I were simply ecstatic. God was manifesting himself through answered prayers again. One evening we had a young lady to come share with our praise team about entering into God's presence and the lifestyle of true worshippers. It was awesome. The young lady began to speak directly to my daughter and told her what God was showing her concerning her singing for the Lord. This young lady also shared with the team about severing unhealthy relationships. This was confirmation of what God has told me concerning her and her ministry in the body of Christ. The next day my daughter and I were riding in the car. She began by saying, "Mom, I am the one who has to sever unhealthy relationships." My daughter went on to tell me that she took care of it after the meeting with the praise team. I wanted to jump out of the car and run up and down the street! I wanted to scream in my loudest voice, "Hallelujah!" However, I had to keep my composure. I said, "That's great. I'm sure God is pleased with what you have done."

Our relationship with our daughter still is very important to us. We longed for the day of having her back. She is now living for God and walking in her purpose. Healing has come forth for her as well as for us. I still read out loud my confession for her. I still thank God daily for her as well as her siblings. I still quote my favorite scripture concerning my daughter, Proverbs 11:21, "...but the seed of the righteous shall be delivered." We are and will continue to stand on God's Word for our daughter.

My prayer is that readers will find hope in the pages in this book. Do not accept what the world says about homosexuality or any situation that does not line up with the Word of God and His plan for you and/or your family. If it is not dealt with, it can create division in your home, marriage, and other children. Our children need for us to stand and fight for them. You have to stand in faith and trust God to be who He says He is. Most importantly, walk in love with everyone. This is what freed our daughter – love. Let us allow God to be seen in the earth through our lives, in Jesus' Name!

Time to be Honest With Myself and God...

"...for the Lord sees not as man sees; man looks on the outward appearance, but the Lord looks on the heart ..." (1 Samuel 16:7).

Just as I appeared to have my relationship with God in order, this situation with my daughter clearly showed that I had left my first love and had pushed God to the back burner of my life. Because God is the only one who can see into the heart, it is easy for us to mask and hide from others. Think about and record the areas of your life that you keep hidden and masked due to insecurities, failures, sin, or your past. As you begin to write, pray and ask God to reveal all areas that need to be healed and restored. There may be things that you were not aware were hindering your walk with God, and Holy Spirit is able to bring truth to you. Do not allow Satan to trick you into believing a lie, when God has given you His Word which is full of truth and life. Do not be afraid to take this journey with God. He already knew where you would be at this moment and has already planned for your deliverance and blessing. Take a step of faith and believe God for full restoration. If God could do this for me, He can do it for you, too!

_____

_____

_____

_____

_____

_____

_____

_____

_____

_____

_____

Confession

I am healed and restored by faith. I will no longer allow my past to dictate my future. I am free and can be used by God to reach out to others. I accept the forgiveness of God and forgive myself. I will no longer carry the burden of my sin and mistakes, but will cast them upon Jesus, because He cares for me. I allow the healing power of God to restore every broken area of my heart and soul. I am free and will no longer operate according to the lies and deceptions of Satan. I am fearfully and wonderfully made by God and accept all of His blessings for my life. I am free and will not be chained by Satan ever again. I operate in the fruits of the spirit, love as Christ loved, and seek the wisdom of God daily. I am the workmanship of God and have been created for good works, which have already been prepared (Ephesians 2:10). I walk by faith and not by sight and have received all eternal blessings that God has prepared for me. I am free, I am free, I am free!

Salvation Only Found in Jesus

In this book, I shared my story of restoration for my daughter and family. Yet, none of this could be possible without having a relationship with God through Jesus Christ. Because I was born again, I was entitled to every promise and blessing of God as a daughter in His family. If you are not born again and have not accepted Jesus as your Lord and Savior, you have the opportunity to do so right now. As long as you remain outside of the family of God, Satan is your spiritual father and is allowed to do whatever he wants in your life and keep you in bondage. But, if you accept Jesus Christ as Lord in your life, you will no longer be associated with the kingdom of darkness and can have all godly, spiritual weapons and promises at your feet. Once you make this decision, your life will never be the same! It will be the best eternal decision you could ever make in life.

All you need to do to accept this free gift, is to confess with your mouth the Lord Jesus and believe in your heart that God raised Him from the dead, and you will be saved (Romans 10:9-10). Speak aloud the following: Father, I am ready to receive the free gift of salvation from You. I believe in my heart and confess that Jesus Christ is Lord. I believe that You raised Him from the dead because You loved me. Please forgive me for my sins and make me whole. Thank you, Father for preparing a place for me with You eternally. Because I believe in You, I am righteous and will not be put to shame. Thank you Father, I am saved!

That's it! Welcome to the family of God, and I hope that this book will continue to bless and minister to you as you walk towards your healing and restoration.

1. In Touch Magazine. In Touch Ministries, Inc. Copyright 2014.

2. www.dictionary.com

3. Easton, M.G. Illustrated Bible Dictionary, Third Edition, published by Thomas Nelson, 1897.